Bears Unplugged

A Screen Free Adventure

Written by
Papa Moose

Illustrated by
William Velasco

ISBN: 978-1-7361781-6-4

Thanks to all of my FB author friends, especially the gang at
Children's Book Authors and Illustrators, for their feedback and support.
And special thanks to the Director ❤.
- **Papa Moose**

I would like to dedicate this illustration work with all my heart and mind to my great
unconditional friend. To the one who has been my strength and help, to the one who illuminates
my path and gives me wisdom every day to carry out each project, guiding me on each page and
in each stroke I make. Thank you God for teaching me and for always being with me.
- **William Velasco**

Also by Papa Moose

More silly, fun adventures!

Bucky the Sweet-Toothed Beaver

Bucky fights his sugar cravings
with the help of his best friend, Bert.

Lou the Big Horned Rhino

A mighty rhino thinks his horn is too big.

Panic at the Pumpkin Patch

Detective Ryan Holiday and his
basset hound Bo investigate
crimes at a pumpkin patch.

Available on Amazon.com

Visit **www.papamoosebooks.com**
for news, sneak previews and FREE activity sheets!

Bears
Unplugged!

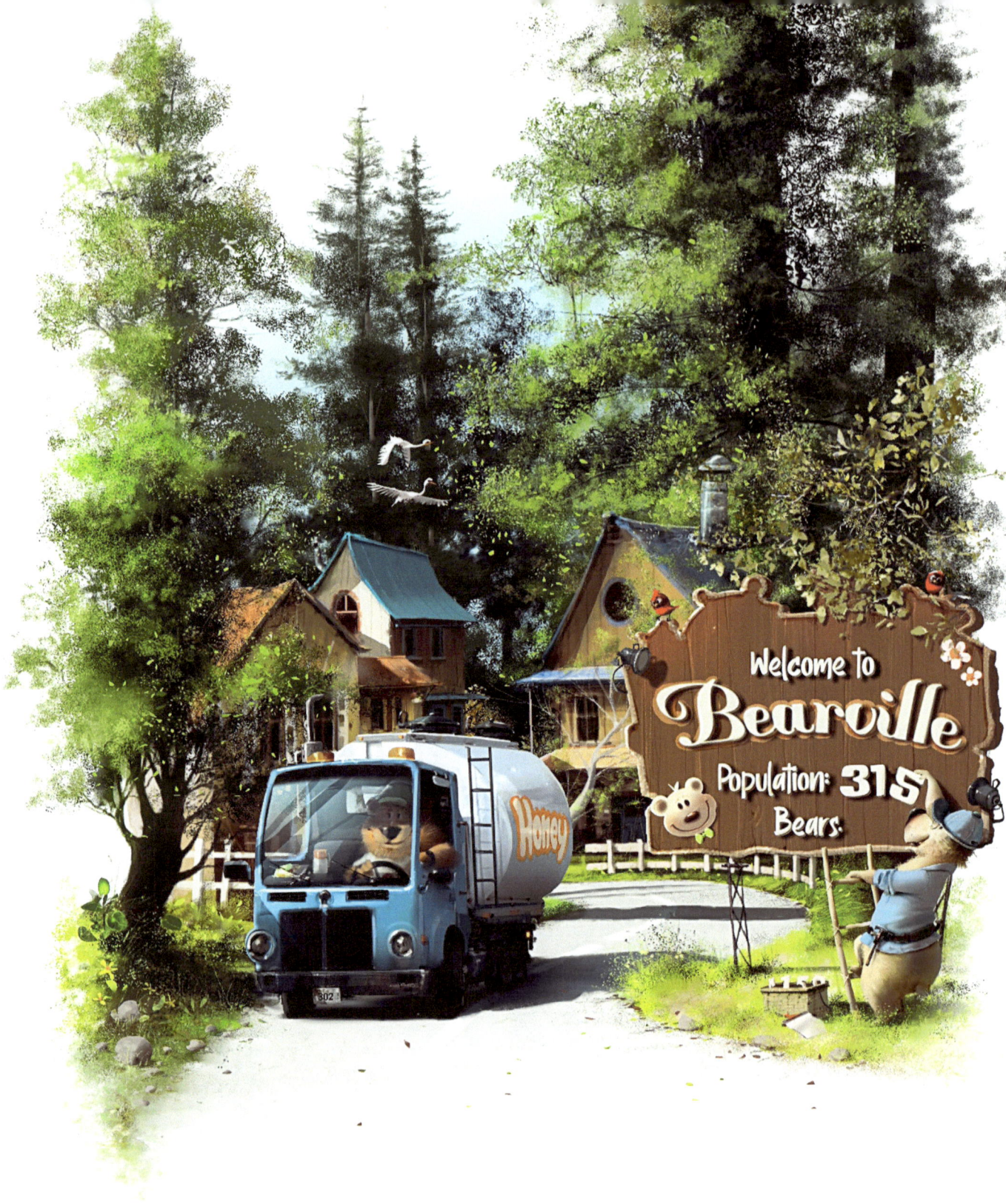

In the woods to the north was a town full of bears,
and they lived without problems, or worries, or cares.

They were all nice and cozy inside of their homes
while they stared at TVs and their gadgets and phones.

Now, it's not like the bears spent their *whole* day online.
There were some other things that they did with their time.

But when worktime was done, every bear in the town
went right back to their screens and would not put them down.

Then one day down in Bearville, much to their surprise,
all their gadgets turned off right in front of their eyes.

There were growls of despair from each store, home and park.
Every bear, young and old, had a screen that was dark.

So the Mayor assembled a noisy town hall
and he said, "I have just had a terrible call.
While I hoped that our internet might be fixed soon,
I am told the repairman won't be here till June!"

Someone cried, "That's three months till our screens are restored!"
And the crowd all complained and they shouted, "We're bored!"

Then a kind grandpa bear slowly rose from his seat.
He was surely the wisest old bear you could meet.
He said, "This is not nearly as bad as it seems,
because I can remember a time without screens.
We were artists! Adventurers!" Grandpa Bear sighed.
"We would talk to each other, and cubs played outside.
So while screens are amazing, they come at a cost
And I think it's too high for the things that we've lost."

The whole crowd listened closely to what Grandpa said.
But they went back to dreaming of screen time instead.
The old bear stood alone as the town shuffled out.
But then Grandpa Bear noticed a young boy named Scout.

"I believe you," Scout said. "It makes great sense to me.
But I really miss playing my games on TV."
"I am sure," Grandpa said. "It is hard when you're blue.
But you know what might help? Why not try something new?"

The next morning in Bearville was quite a sad scene
as the bears sat around, each one missing their screen.

But then some of them saw a most curious sight:
little Scout was outside and was flying a kite!

Pretty soon lots of bear cubs were gathered around
and the parks and the playgrounds filled up with the sound
of a whole group of children out having some fun
as they made up adventures and played in the sun.

Then the grown-ups decided to make a change, too
and to try out new things that they wanted to do.

There was lots of excitement if you were a bear.
There were interesting things going on everywhere.

There were shows starring puppets they knitted by hand.

There were bears who performed in a cool polka band.

There was one bear who pulled rabbits out of a hat.

While another did stunts with his daredevil cat.

Even bears who were lazy and tended to slouch
got a lot more involved when they got off the couch.

As for me, I write stories. Real stories, it's true.
And you're reading the story that I wrote for you.
There are lots of good lessons I wanted to share.
Even if you're a person instead of a bear.

Go outside. Look around.
Leave your screens on the shelf.
Then go out and discover the world for yourself.

For you see, though at last all the power returned,
in the months in between, this is what we had learned:
that our screens were connected, but we'd grown apart
till that magical spring when we made a new start.

Yes, we still use our gadgets and gizmos and such.
But not nearly as often. Not nearly as much.

There is so much more fun to be had with your time.
It's a wonderful life when you live it offline.

www.ingramcontent.com/pod-product-compliance
Lightning Source LLC
Chambersburg PA
CBHW042127040426
42450CB00002B/98